POINTERS
TO
PRESENCE

Shaykh Fadhlalla Haeri

ZAHRA PUBLICATIONS

Published by Zahra Publications

PO Box 50764
Wierda Park 0149
Centurion
South Africa

email info@sfhfoundation.com
www.sfhfoundation.com
www.zahrapublications.com

© 2013 Shaykh Fadhlalla Haeri
All rights reserved. No part of this book may be reproduced or utilised in any form or by any means, electronic or mechanical, without permission in writing from the publisher.

Designed and typeset in South Africa by Mizpah

To purchase an eBook version of this booklet, please visit www.zahrapublications.com

ISBN 978-1-919826-70-7

Acknowledgements

The author would like to thank Leyya Kalla for compiling and producing this booklet in March 2013, which has been republished and produced again in July 2019.

About the Author

Born in Karbala, Iraq, Shaykh Fadhlalla Haeri, comes from several generations of religious and spiritual leaders. After several years living and working in the west, he rediscovered the universal relevance of the Qur'an and Islamic teachings for our present day. His emphasis has been on transformative worship and refinement of conduct, as preludes to the realisation of the prevalence of Divine grace. He considers that the purpose of life is to know and resonate with the eternal essence of the one and only Lifegiver — Allah.

Contents

Introduction	1
1. Self-Evolvement & Conduct	3
2. Cycles of Life & Death	15
3. Dualities, the Seen & Unseen	27
4. Relationships & Love	39
5. Governance & Leadership	49
6. Knowledge & Science	57
7. Religion & Spirituality	69
8. Liberation & Enlightenment	77

Introduction

'Pointers to Presence' is an elixir for hearts seeking truth. This collection of aphorisms by Shaykh Fadhlalla Haeri provides insights and openings into higher consciousness and spirituality.

This collection attempts to answer the questions posed by a curious person or serious seeker regarding the meaning of life. It addresses a wide range of issues including self-conduct, governance, leadership, religion and spirituality, i.e. a condensed 'map' for living lucidly in the present.

The author takes the liberty in the text to coin some terms that may help to convey subtle issues in life.

1. Self-Evolvement & Conduct

The most challenging issue in human existence is to understand the nature of the self itself. Some of the most frequently asked questions are "Who am I?", and "What can I do to be content and happy?" Some people are naturally endowed with a healthy disposition from early on in life and seem to attract positive outcomes. For others, a better knowledge of the relationship between one's ego and the higher self are necessary. Life and its quality are related to the extent of our ability to refer to higher consciousness within ourselves.

The following section includes aphorisms covering the self and its emergence, the interplay between self and soul, behavior and conduct, and other personality dynamics.

What is good for you? Sometimes you think you know but often are uncertain. This is because you don't know who you really are!

Most human struggles are about attaining the state of being in paradise—where no needs exist and where states are ever content and happy.

What does it mean to be you? The ego-self is so elusive and tricky that it can only be known by the light of your perfect soul.

When a traveller is lost, he is presented with an opportunity to discover where, why and who it is that is lost.

The illusion of the 'self' or the 'ego' is a necessary start to realising its 'phantom' reality—a shadow, which hides the inner light.

The self is a reflection of the soul upon the developing person and contains aspects of the past and present, illumined by the soul.

The self always creates its own illusions of a separate existence, beyond which lies perfect transcendence.

The true self is the eternal soul, and not what we are deluded by.

When self-concern becomes extreme, it brings about its own self-destruction.

A crisis of identity could be the unlocking of destiny's door to Reality. Welcome the crisis as a new dawn, be patient, and witness all.

The self is a companion shadow of the soul but desires independence.

The soul is never in doubt: it knows its own perfect nature.

Real self-growth means soul-connection
and liberation from the animal self.

The desire to appear 'good' is a
subconscious attempt not to disgrace the
soul's perfection.

Spiritual awakening and clear vision
of Reality happens when the fog of the
lower self is lifted.

The hidden soul shines when the self is
groomed and disciplined.

Rebellion relates to the self, expressing its illusion of individuality and special independent identity.

Guilt is the discrepancy between what had been done and what could have been done better.

The self always tries to assert its own authority in whatever way is possible, and that includes acting irrationally and confusedly.

The desire to be different and special is an expression of dissatisfaction with one's inner present state.

Desires and attachments increase limited, basic conditioned awareness and reduce higher consciousness.

Blame and denial are natural defenses of the ego in perpetuating its shadowy reality.

Desires are expressions of what is perceived as agreeable or required for contentment and a good life.

Attachment is a feeling that enhances the perception of well-beingness or happiness.

Personality and character relate to intentions and actions, as well as genetic origin and the environment.

'Good' character relates generally to what brings about goodness and harmony. The reverse is what causes disturbance and conflict.

Calling a person 'good' or 'bad' simply relates to the person's intentions and actions, which can change.

Aggression, fear and sorrow will continue as long as we remain concerned for survival and fear death.

Hatred, fear and animosity toward a perceived enemy mask any goodness that may emanate indirectly from them.

The soul's light is veiled behind layers of fear, anger, ambition, desires and other shadows of the ego.

Shyness is a result of uncertainty that faces one in a particular situation. Confidence is what removes it.

The self will be depressed when ignored, excluded or reprimanded. The self always fears the loss of its 'deluded' identity.

A sound mind is necessary for discernment, correct judgment and wisdom. It is the pure heart that allows the light of the soul to lead us to the inner gardens of joy.

Mind and intellect are great worldly assets but without the light of the soul they can only lead to misery and disappointment.

The mind's nature is not stillness as it continuously seeks to connect and relate the inner with the outer world.

The self fears and resists mindlessness; like every creation, it is programmed to assert its identity.

The lower self is naturally connected to earthly issues or subjects. The story is complete when the self and the soul are in unison.

The human mind needs training, discipline and focus to become an evolved mind. This leads to higher intellect, creativity and inspiration.

Every person has a mind and heart. The mind deals with rationality and reason, the heart with passion and spiritual awakening. One is for differentiation and the other is for unification.

Short term pleasures are enticements for real joy, which relates to higher consciousness.

There is constancy in our care for our personal condition, as well as to the group to which we belong. The outer objective may change in form and appearance but the ultimate destination is ever constant and is towards truth and the Supreme Consciousness or God.

What we understand of consciousness is what is limited or conditioned, such as pain or pleasure. Pure consciousness can only be felt in deep meditation, where no mental activity or self-awareness exists.

2. CYCLES OF LIFE & DEATH

The entire universe ebbs and flows according to rhythms and frequencies, which appear as cycles and follow special patterns. As human beings we are always challenged by the meaning of life and nature of death. We always look for new stimulation and get bored with whatever is familiar. In truth we are looking for an ever present mystery, our soul, or spirit or God!

The following section includes aphorisms covering these various states and transitions of life.

Your mood may change any moment! Yet your soul is ever constant and reliable, if only you were to lose yourself in it!

Disappointments and mistakes will teach us to be more focused towards appropriate and feasible appointments.

Earthly life is like a net we weave around ourselves. Whatever more we do entraps us further.

Depression occurs when you are not being joyful or content. It means you need to re-calibrate your attitude, emotions and inner presence.

Nostalgia and melancholy are the mists and smoke that veil us from witnessing a joyful state. This is wrongfully perceived as being lost.

Despair arises when depression is accompanied by loss of hope for a better outcome. The ego fears its death!

The self struggles for recognition, status and honor, all of which it can never fully attain. The ego is in constant turmoil, until it loses its identity completely.

Pride is an expression of the desire to be given special status or position.

It is the ego that is the cause of most suffering, whereas the soul or spirit exudes wondrous spiritual offerings.

To exaggerate is an attempt to highlight the importance of an issue.

No one wants to miss out on goodness and everyone tries to avoid misery.

Whatever is new appears special until familiarity makes it ordinary.

The desire for death indicates the darkness of the self and deprivation of the light of the soul.

The flow of time creates the idea of achievement, attainment, a sense of purpose and direction in life.

The flow of life enables us to understand, change and evolve in consciousness.

Pure Consciousness is utterly free from all limitations, whereas its offspring - limited or conditioned consciousness - is defined by birth and death.

The real nature of the moment is timelessness and pure consciousness.

Life and death represent a temporary connection between what has its origin before time - the soul - and what belongs to time - the self.

A personal life presents us with a sample of eternal and infinite life—the soul within the heart.

The desire to prolong life is due to the need to experience the eternal presence of life itself.

Life is a love affair; and death, therefore, appears as a tragedy, until one realises how eternal this affair really is!

Death is nature's loyalty to the original Unity. The material body returns to its mother earth and the soul returns to the infinite ocean of spiritual lights.

Whilst alive our behavior evolves from a most basic animal level towards higher consciousness. After death our soul carries traces of the lower self, in its ongoing journey.

Death lifts the veil upon eternity.

When personal life has led to the realisation of the eternal and perfect nature of the soul, then no fear or sorrow can tarnish life's joys.

At the beginning and at the end of an event time seems to move faster. At the beginning of creation events moved at great speed. The same is expected at the end.

The hereafter is already here and now, for eternity is not subject to place and time.

The universe and all of creation occurs within the framework of space and time. It is the scales of quantity and quality that change.

The mystery of life is neither solvable nor teachable. It is only livable after giving into it - a move from 'becoming' to 'being'.

Whatever is created is rushing towards its destiny, where it emerged from in the first place.

The idea that life is worth living will help in creating the belief that it is worth living. Life itself does not need any affirmation.

Existence is a spiritual trap. The only way out of it is by progressing in awareness from form to meaning, then to essence and Oneness.

Lasting happiness is a natural outcome of being with the constant bliss of Supreme Consciousness.

Higher consciousness is behind every level of conditioned consciousness; all of which aspire towards higher consciousness.

Once the seeker is established in higher consciousness, there is no going back. He then needs to let go of all personal choices or possibilities.

The sun that appears to set on one horizon is rising upon another. Such is the cycle of birth and death.

When you are consumed by your principle duty in life, your rewards are given to you unconditionally.

Fear of death is due to attachments to earthly desires or ignorance of the immortal soul.

Reason, scepticism and rationality are all myths, when seen through the lens of Reality.

For many people the past is a burden that causes the future to become confused and unwelcome.

Life may be considered short, yet it starts from 'no time' and returns to infinity again.

It is a great fortune to be joyful in the twilight years without fear of death. This happens as a result of living a life of good intentions, actions and being blessed by grace.

Life's journey begins in wonder and surprise. It ends with witnessing realities and Truth. In between, we are relentlessly challenged and oscillate between fear and hope.

3. DUALITIES, THE SEEN & UNSEEN

Whatever we observe or experience is one of two complementary opposites. Morality and virtues are simple outcomes of turning away from vices and ignorance. All values have their opposites. Every truth has within it the seed of falsehood. Whatever we consider to be rational and real is close to the unreal. Truth is the source of the entire universe and from It, all other transient realities emanate and return.

The aphorisms in this section relate to these dualities, mysteries of Oneness, hope and fear, and good and bad values.

The primary source of creation is a mysterious Oneness.

What we experience are our intentions and the contents of our actions.

Otherness is a camouflaged aspect of Oneness.

Deceptions are part of earthly realities, which are all in themselves veils of the One Reality.

What is good is also beautiful, but not everything that appears beautiful is good.

That which is ever-present seems ever-absent to human sight—Allah!

Positive thinking is the other side of negative thinking. Neither way has durability or reliability.

The greater the outer difficulties or failures, the more profound can be one's submission to Reality.

Whatever is near you in form may be far from you in meaning, and whatever is far from you in form may be near in meaning.

Sometimes the truth seems far, other times it is close. Our life is a work in progress, from Truth and back to It.

To look at life through the lens of the soul is to experience the seamlessness of what is transient and what is eternal.

Mind and senses are there to realise dualities and learn discrimination and wisdom.

Existence is held by the space-time continuum, but life spans both this realm as well as boundlessness.

A breakthrough in perception can often occur after a great shock, grief or relief.

All has emerged from the unseen; to the same unseen source, all will return. The same One Source is ever-present.

Dualities sometimes meet and complement each other, while at other times clash and nullify each other. At all times the outcome is Unity.

Hope is the promise of desirable future possibilities; a good illusion that gives a purpose to earthly life.

You may deceive many, except your own conscience or soul.

Attraction is toward Unity and repulsion is turning away from it. Both attraction and repulsion have emanated from the original Oneness.

Fear is rooted in possible changes that may disturb or end what is perceived as goodness or happiness.

Human drives become neutralised with the disappearance of dualities in the light of Oneness.

The drive for Oneness is relentless; from specific perfect connections and relationships, to pure perfection with no otherness.

Most lies come to life due to a spark of truth that accompanies them.

Intuition and insights abound when the personal view is not obstructing the soul's intuitions.

The joyful freedom of losing 'I'-dentity follows the hardship of having gained one in the first place.

The bee may consider the flower to exist for its own sake. The nectar is the flower's means to propagate and replicate ongoingness and eternity.

Whatever is created gives some idea of its end at its beginning.

There is a natural tendency in us to reject limitations, for our life force emanates from a limitless Reality.

Fear helps human consciousness to be focused on hope; appropriate intention and action will expand consciousness.

Absolute Truth is such an immense force that it can only manifest with dualities, veils and shadows. This is the nature of our world.

Our love for what is constant regulates what is by nature subject to change. We are caught in the earthly realm, longing for what is heavenly.

When attention is directed towards higher consciousness then personal feelings become insignificant - the self becomes lost unto the soul.

Accepting limitations, as well as sensing, feeling and meditating upon the Limitless, will bring about a balanced perspective in life.

Natural sounds and harmonious music can help us transcend the lower self towards higher consciousness. Meditation also helps this transcendence.

We experience life as we really are at heart, not as we imagine ourselves to be. The world is an honest mirror, reflecting our inner state.

To give up is to deny duality and its limited reality. What is needed is to realise their source of Oneness.

Close to origin, differentiation ceases,
as does thoughts of otherness and
separation. At Oneness all else vanishes.

Rejecting worldly limitations doesn't lead
to limitlessness but merely to greater
divides and confusions. Infinity is an
attribute of the absolute Reality, not
earthly creations.

God is the Reality, which is the source of
all beings, and permeates everything in
the universe, seen and unseen.

Time and space can hold infinite varieties
of entities that have simply emerged
from Oneness.

Human life is balanced between fear and hope. We avoid and fear what is perceived as bad and are drawn by hope to what is considered desirable for happiness.

4. RELATIONSHIPS & LOVE

The mystery of what holds the universe together can be partially understood when we realise the interconnectedness of all that is seen and unseen. All causes and effects are discernible by our minds. Subtler connections relate to the subtler world and the soul. Love is the cosmic force that unifies diverse forces or entities.

This section looks at relationships, love, passion and connections.

Our hope for love that lasts is a sample of the love of the eternal Truth.

The heart is pained whenever connections are severed or the light of Oneness is dimmed.

The outer world is the human nursery for evolvement and growth. Our lessons are learnt through interactions and relationships.

A mature rational mind is a helpful worldly reference, whereas the purified heart reflects Truth.

The soul within the heart transmits the unifying light, which appears as love.

Love may begin as exclusive or specific - the love of a mother for her baby. All love leads to the ocean of Love's universal inclusivity.

Love is a power that gushes out of the heart and overrules the head, reason and normal behavior.

Love makes an ordinary person feel special, unique and elevated above the usual state of consciousness, with its concerns and worries.

Love places you in a transient zone
between self and soul.

Relationships make the self feel
connected, important and secure.

The love of self is a minor reflection of
the love of the soul— the source of all
love. Self-love is due to love of the soul,
for how can anyone love meanness of
the self?

Every love is a quest for Oneness.

The lover is blind to the faults and shortcomings of the beloved, who is perceived as ever-perfect.

Human love is a sample of the unconditional Divine love that emanates from the essence of creation and governs the universe.

When you lose yourself totally, love will emerge from the clouds of fear and concerns.

Love connects and unites different people, who are from diverse roots and cultures.

Love gives rise to loyalty, honesty, generosity, compassion, kindness, friendship and concern, amongst other virtues.

Human friendship, compatibility and love describe different levels of unity and harmony.

When head and heart are united in a person, the resulting peace and equilibrium can influence others towards a balanced life.

When love is unconditional it is most powerful. The human version is often tarnished with expectations, judgments and fears.

Love is nature's most dominant unifying force. Hatred is its opposite.

Love is the unifying grace that engulfs the universe and connects diverse forces and entities.

What unifies can also divide: consider religion, ideology, money, blood relationships, business and sport.

In most modern urban communities, poverty can be a major cause of stress and breakdowns in relationships.

The sage may heal effectively by simply listening to the sicknesses of the heart, rather than focusing on the patient's complaints.

Companionship shapes the behavior of a child, and invariably influences the adolescent. The mature and wise adult however, is less affected.

Money can remove poverty and some misery but it does not guarantee happiness.

Human beings need to communicate and express themselves. Ultimately it is the soul which expresses its grace.

A relationship endures and thrives if each partner helps the other to achieve their maximum human and spiritual potential.

Every entity that exists expresses its nature in obvious and subtle ways. Rain causes water to flow, a fire burns, and a rose dispenses perfume.

Our life flourishes when we connect through empathy, sympathy, sharing and caring. Isolation may help us to heal but not to grow and evolve.

We are driven to experience new aspects of consciousness until we arrive at the door of Supreme Consciousness - the Source of All.

Serving and giving to others are steps that help the lower self evolve towards its soul. It is through selfless acts that we experience soulfulness.

5. Governance & Leadership

Human beings cannot thrive in isolation. We learn through the mirroring of others, and are influenced by our environment and socio-cultural background. Good governance will help a society evolve towards their highest potential. Outer differences will fade away as we realise that we share the same needs, desires and hopes. With clarity of mind and heart, good intentions and appropriate actions, progress will be visible and the quality of civilisation will improve.

Here we look at issues of power, influence, respect, culture, authority and leadership.

Political aspirations are the natural desire to be looked up to, admired and followed. As the soul is, the self desires to be.

Power lies in the ability to control a situation and alter the course of events. This power is contained within the soul and the self can access it through transcendence.

A villain or a hero is produced by outer temptations interacting with inner tendencies and ego drives.

All forces and energies emanate from one Sublime Source and return to It.

A heroic act implies courage, generosity
of spirit, selflessness and timely action,
with least concern or fear about outcome.

We love power and to be near its source,
yet we are least aware of the powerful
soul within our own heart.

It is natural for a healthy, ambitious
person to change the world. The
wise person's priority is to change
himself first.

Civilisations flourish due to evolving
consciousness and are protected by
humane laws that ensure goodness.

The self resents authority, until it experiences real benefit from it, such as knowledge, wisdom and well-beingness.

Outer knowledge is essential for worldly success, and self-knowledge for spiritual success.

An artist aspires for a masterpiece; a philosopher for ideas that could help mankind to live a better life, the sage lives with his sacred soul that is the source of eternal bliss.

Suffering is mostly self-inflicted and is due to confusion and ignorance.

Friendship expresses similarities and agreeable connections. Animosity expresses repulsion, fear, and hatred.

Any action motivated by the ego or the lower self will hinder progress towards experiencing higher consciousness.

An action may appear to be generous or good, yet it leads to disappointment and misery. Reading the map of reality is essential for arrival at a good destination.

Every action is energised by deep intention and the attention that accompanies it.

Worldly plans and actions aim for a good outcome. Spiritual life realises perfection in all situations.

Earthly peace is when nature is least disturbed by human will and interference. Spiritual peace is when movement, thought and action are stilled.

Outer peace can only be sustained when inner peace is attained.

Our evolution and progress in life is according to the quality and effect of our actions and deeds. Creation emanated from a state of sacred stillness and peace. This is why we all yearn for lasting Peace.

For the wise, duty and service take precedence over personal desires.

Wealth is an aspect of power: for most people it is to be acquired. A few witness it as a life force that will test and afflict whoever is engulfed by the earthly domain and lacks any spiritual insight.

Politics are local in implementation, universal in principle.

Cultural vitality is due to the exchange of ideas and products with other peoples and cultures.

For survival of the young, outer care and authority is needed. For maturity and evolvement we need spiritual light and guidance.

6. KNOWLEDGE & SCIENCE

Curiosity and the constant drive to explore and know is a natural trait in all human beings. We desire knowledge and wisdom in order to reduce mistakes and disappointments. We hope to prolong whatever good experiences we have. Time is relative and we wonder about the nature of timelessness and the hereafter. The universe is experienced through the constraints of space and time. Science has helped to show numerous levels of interconnectedness.

In this section the aphorisms relate to knowledge, wisdom, truth, time and eternity.

Whoever sees himself as a teacher
of spirituality is not fit to teach.
Whoever desires to be a leader
may not be fit to lead.

If you desire illumination, then you need
to leave behind whatever has to do with
mind or creation.

To understand the past is a necessary
step to escape what is undesirable
in the present.

We are at ease with what is familiar and
known, and curious or apprehensive
about what is unknown.

It is natural for a mature person to desire mindlessness and the vastness of the state beyond 'normal' consciousness.

All questions and answers are connected and neutralise each other. The answers, however, are always there waiting for the question to let them emerge.

The origin is One and so is the destination. Questions and answers were in unity before separation into duality.

The fruit of knowledge is that which fuels the quest for further knowledge.

Forms and shapes have inner meaning.
This gives them their separate identity.

The answer becomes evident, when the
need becomes pressing and urgent.

The desire to know the root and cause of
everything comes from our innate drive
to comprehend that which is beyond
the boundaries of space and time -
the Origin of all.

Gnosis is the knowledge that one has
neither independent existence in life, nor
any separation from Truth.

Truth is beyond anything that exists, yet sheds light upon everything that exists.

Ideas and thoughts are sparks that emanate and are coloured by the mind, which places them within the frame of space and time.

The human soul is the source cause of one's life. Its departure upon death is the proof of its existence.

A sage defines Truth as being able 'to see through the eye of God'. We all need to experience that truth.

The sage has forsaken all earthly valuables and possessions; he has gained the spiritual treasury and eternal bliss.

Peace arises when tranquility and stillness reign; movement is where agitation and turmoil reign.

The silence of a sage may convey much more than a discourse.

An enlightened person may have shed earthly desires and attachments, but is still driven to reflect the original light and delight of Oneness.

All movement and change are earthly veils of the constant eternal Truth. With a still mind and pure heart the soul's perfection will shine forth.

The light of Truth will illume the shadows of uncertainties and confusions.

Eternal Truth bestows a temporary legitimacy on all that is transient and temporary—all of existence and what is transient in creation.

Timelessness is liberation from being caught between the past and the future. Presence contains the key to that liberation.

Truth is the absolute light that shines from behind its own colourful covers and shades.

Divine Reality produces and energises infinite varieties of realities. Every experience or state has a temporary reality that has emanated from the Real.

Faith is the belief that truth will be discovered. When that happens we call it enlightenment.

The origin of life is eternal and every person's life is drawn from the same Source. The discovery of that truth is the purpose of life.

If time is considered valuable, then eternity must be an infinite treasure.

Truth is realised beyond mindlessness and through the purified heart.

Human beings are but guests in this world. It is our privilege to acknowledge this truth to the most magnificent and generous Host.

To pursue knowledge is like making a candle. Living by knowledge is like seeing by the light of the candle.

The enlightened person is aware of the immediate presence of paradise within.

The philosopher's stone was the alchemist's quest to transform lead into gold. To realise the eternal nature of an instant is more valuable than all treasures.

Supreme Consciousness is eternal and cannot be defined by our limited consciousness.

When you wake up from a nightmare you would rather forget it; similarly an enlightened person hardly recalls his past.

Most people struggle to exercise their own will. The sage is free from personal free will as he lives in the eternal moment.

Truth is self-evident and can only be realised by itself, in endless varieties and to limitless extents.

Demonstrable facts are the foundations of physical and material sciences, whilst faith opens the door to metaphysics.

7. Religion & Spirituality

The human tendency to investigate the origin of life and the nature of God is deeply ingrained in us. Religions have helped in human evolvement, social cohesion and the establishment of moral norms. They have also been used to justify wars and discord.

The ultimate purpose of prayers, meditation and contemplation is to access Supreme Consciousness, from which other levels of consciousness emanate—thereby gaining a better quality of life.

This section includes aphorisms relating to choice, religion and spirituality.

Outer boundaries and restrictions are necessary steps before insights to inner limitlessness are discovered.

Religions reflect people's need for prescriptions that help them to relate what is earthly and rational to the heavenly unseen perfections.

If you are seeking the sacred, then look deeply into the secular; to understand the secular, discover the sacred within it. They are two aspects of Oneness.

Supplication and prayer are expressions of personal hopes and aspirations, some of which are realistic, others fantasies.

Religions are paths to perfect conduct and realisation of the eternal truth. They are not rigid rituals and laws.

We live and experience the world of cause and effect, whereas spiritual wisdom leads us to pure consciousness which is beyond the mind and intellect.

You may not be able to know your soul but you can always benefit from its guidance and light, if you listen to it.

You are a realised being by virtue of your soul. Confusion is due to your ego.

The greatest inner wealth is the knowledge of your dependency upon your soul, which can only lead you back to paradise.

Life's experiences can reveal to us the veils of the ego and lead us to towards the inner light.

The best choice is not one of two; it is simply becoming one with the moment and witnessing perfect reality here and now—every instant.

Unjust actions produce misery, conflict and confusion. Just actions will lead to wisdom and good life.

Choice is confusion. It ends when you know what the correct course of action is. Goodness is only one choice.

To abandon personal choice may lead to life without confusion or suffering.

The greater is the knowledge of the Real, the deeper is contentment and joy.

When culture or religions do not lead to spirituality and enlightenment, they will degenerate and disintegrate.

The less there is of self-concern, the greater the potential for soul-awareness and higher consciousness.

When information causes reformation then it may lead to transformation.

There are as many paths to the Truth as there are human beings; every self has the illusion of its own identity and direction in life.

When you pray with your innermost heart, you are at the door where the answer already awaits you.

Selfless service and charitable acts are minor reflections of the Real source of generosity, mercy and grace—the One.

Whatever you think or do will leave its trace on your life and influence your future state.

Whoever considers himself godly, he may be the furthest from the truth.

8. Liberation & Enlightenment

When basic needs for survival are fulfilled, we naturally look for beauty, harmony and higher values in life. For thousands of years philosophers have reflected upon human needs and drives. They have concluded that what we desire is liberation from confusion and ignorance, and the realisation of universal connectedness, ultimately Oneness. Today's scientists postulate that before the big bang there was a singularity and after the big collapse all returns to it. The ancient sages have all sung the tune of Oneness and attributed lasting happiness to the realisation of that Truth.

This last section includes aphorisms relating to beauty, peace, harmony, happiness and grace.

Asceticism is when you know that you cannot own anything. Liberation is when nothing owns or controls you.

To stop and die is to start and be.

Lasting freedom lies beyond the emotional swings of earthly dualities, like fear and sorrow, love and hate, good and bad, I and others, true and false.

Freedom implies neutrality, harmony and peace, inwardly within oneself and outwardly in witnessing creation.

The nature of knowledge is a light that overflows as a grace from the Divine source.

The hierarchy in the quest for freedom begins with the outer, physical and material, then mental, and ultimately freedom at heart.

The universe emerged from Oneness and is sustained by It.

Whoever has experienced the truth of Oneness wishes to make that wonderful experience accessible to others.

Liberation occurs when personal conditioned consciousness merges with Supreme Consciousness.

When there is nothing to be done, the act of witnessing fills the possibilities of all intentions and actions.

Liberation is the outcome of the transcendence of the mind and its limitations.

Pure space lies beyond emptiness or fullness.

Separation and distance from creation is the first step toward realising nearness and Oneness.

Whether attracted to a direction or repulsed by it, at all times you are drawn towards Oneness. Wherever you turn, Truth is facing you.

Lasting happiness is beyond tranquility, ease and harmony. It is based upon perfect contentment, irrespective of the relationship with the outer world and with one's own self.

The seeds of the future are sown by every thought, intention and action.

Happiness begins to be experienced when you forget yourself and have no self-concerns.

Small pleasures are little windows upon the vast garden of joy, where pleasures and displeasures disappear into the ocean of perfect bliss.

Pleasures are balanced by displeasure, but real happiness is dependent upon inner contentment and joy, far removed from outer change and uncertainty.

An enlightened being experiences perfection at all levels, beyond all limitations and mindsets.

A fruit plucked from a tree in the wilderness may taste better than any bought in a shop. Our soul is the ultimate free gift and race.

The present is ever constant. The heart lives in the now, whereas the mind lives in time, always changing.

We love to have more time and eternal life. Presence is beyond time and place.

What is good and appropriate is that which is least disturbing, or what helps stability and ongoingness.

When you have no outer fears or hopes
then you are at the door of the infinite
treasures of Presence.

Our delight in good endings represents
our drive to experience and witness
perfection.

Perfection is ever-present, irrespective
of one's personal state or feelings.
Once all personal illusions are stopped,
the perfection of the moment
reveals itself clearly.

Every moment emerges from perfect
timelessness and reflects that grace.

A tragedy becomes a comedy when viewed through the lens of unity.

Your contact with reality carries the imprint of the infinite.

Presence is the Divine attribute that beams grace and joy.

Presence clearly announces Itself, when absence vanishes.

Take care of your earthly issues and trust in the heavenly perfections, which also contain the earthly.

Your hopes and fears prevent you from witnessing the sacred perfection—universally prevalent, always near.

Your future destiny will be perfect, if you realise the perfection of the moment.

Whoever realises the perfection of the moment, will reconcile with whatever destiny is experienced.

We adore beauty, peace, and harmony because they are attributes of Supreme Consciousness. We love whatever reminds us of the One.

www.ingramcontent.com/pod-product-compliance
Lightning Source LLC
Chambersburg PA
CBHW060209050426
42446CB00013B/3029